The
Kennedys

by
Cass R. Sandak

CRESTWOOD HOUSE
New York

Maxwell Macmillan Canada
Toronto

Maxwell Macmillan International
New York Oxford Singapore Sydney

Library of Congress Cataloging-in-Publication Data
Sandak, Cass R.
    The Kennedys / by Cass R. Sandak. — 1st ed.
      p. cm. — (First families)
    Summary: Presents the life of John F. Kennedy and his family, with emphasis on his years as president.
    ISBN 0-89686-633-5
    1. Kennedy, John F. (John Fitzgerald), 1917–1963—Family—Juvenile literature. 2. Kennedy family—Juvenile literature. 3. Presidents—United States—Biography—Juvenile literature. [1. Kennedy, John F. (John Fitzgerald), 1917–1963. 2. Kennedy family. 3. Presidents.] I. Title. II. Series: Sandak, Cass R. First families.
E842.Z9S26   1991
973.922'092—dc20
[B]   91-2911
                                                  CIP
                                                  AC

Photo Credits
Cover photo courtesy of the John Fitzgerald Kennedy Library
AP—Wide World Photos: 4, 13, 17, 18, 20, 29, 30, 31, 37, 39, 42, 43
John Fitzgerald Kennedy Library: 9, 14, 23, 27, 33, 34
The Bettmann Archive: 40

CRESTWOOD HOUSE

Macmillan Publishing Company
866 Third Avenue
New York, NY 10022

Maxwell Macmillan Canada, Inc.
1200 Eglinton Avenue East
Suite 200
Don Mills, Ontario M3C 3N1

Macmillan Publishing Company is part of the Maxwell Communication Group of Companies.

Produced by Flying Fish Studio

Printed in the United States of America

First edition

10 9 8 7 6 5 4 3 2 1

CONTENTS

A Fatal Friday...5

Young Jack..6

JFK in World War II..10

The Young Jackie..12

The Road to the White House......................................14

The 1960 Campaign...18

The Inauguration..21

The Beautiful Couple..22

JFK in the Oval Office..25

The Lively First Family...30

The White House Restoration......................................35

A Typical Day...36

The Funeral...38

The Legacy of JFK 41

Jackie After JFK 41

Camelot...43

For Further Reading...45

Index...47

The Kennedy motorcade shortly after the president was shot. The white arrow points to Kennedy's foot. The black arrow points to Mrs. John Connally, wife of the Texas governor.

A Fatal Friday

Almost any American who was alive on November 22, 1963, remembers the day with shocking clarity. It was a Friday, it was just after 1:30 in the afternoon on the East Coast, when the awful news came. John F. Kennedy had been shot. Around noontime in Texas, a motorcade had been making its way from Dallas's Love Field. Shots had rung out. Secret Serviceman Clint Hill was the first to reach the car after the shooting. President Kennedy turned around briefly. Then he slumped onto his wife Jackie's lap. She threw herself over his body as if to protect him. The car sped out of the motorcade toward Parkland Memorial Hospital for help.

The news was sporadic and unclear. An hour went by before anything was known for sure. But the minutes seemed like a lifetime. Finally it was clear. Kennedy had died soon after the shots had pierced his head. A young life and a brief presidency were over.

And a family hope that had been born almost 50 years before was dashed.

Young Jack

John Fitzgerald Kennedy was descended from Irish immigrants on both sides of his family. His mother was Rose Fitzgerald. She was the daughter of John F. Fitzgerald, or "Honey Fitz," who was mayor of Boston around the turn of the century. Jack's father, Joseph Patrick, was the grandson of Patrick Kennedy. He was the Kennedy who had come to Boston in the 1840s from Ireland to escape the great potato famine.

John Fitzgerald Kennedy was born in Brookline, Massachusetts, on May 29, 1917. He was the second oldest in a family of nine children. Joe Junior had been born in 1915. It was on Joe Junior that Joseph Senior pinned his hopes. There was no question: His son Joe would become president. After Jack came Rosemary (1918), Kathleen (1920), Eunice (1921), Patricia (1924), Robert (1925), Jean (1928) and Edward, or Ted, (1932).

Both of Kennedy's grandfathers had been active politicians in Massachusetts. Patrick Joseph Kennedy had served in both houses of the state legislature. And Honey Fitz served in the U.S. Congress before becoming Boston's third Irish-American mayor.

Jack's father, Joseph, made a fortune, first in banking and then in Chicago real estate. He also made a killing in liquor sales following the repeal of Prohibition. He was named U.S. Ambassador to the Court of St. James's in the late 1930s. All the Kennedy children joined him in London during this historic time. And they were there when World War II broke out in September 1939.

John Kennedy's mother, Rose, was blessed with a firm Catholic faith and remarkable energy. She was already 70 when she campaigned for her son in his bid for the presidency. And she was able to fully enjoy seeing him in the White House. She was often a guest at White House functions. In 1990 she celebrated her 100th birthday.

The house where Jack Kennedy was born was a modest gray-shingle home. It soon became too small for the growing clan. Jack Kennedy was only four years old when the family moved to a larger house nearby. And when he was ten they moved to the fashionable Riverdale section of the Bronx, just north of Manhattan.

John F. Kennedy was baptized at St. Aidan's Catholic Church in Brookline. He also served as an altar boy there. The family was still living in Brookline when Jack entered the Dexter School, which his older brother, Joseph, also attended. For a short time before, Jack had gone to a public school in Brookline.

From 1931 to 1935 Jack attended Choate. It is one of New England's most distinguished preparatory schools. In 1935 Jack entered Princeton, but illness forced him to drop out before Christmas. In September 1936 he entered Harvard. During much of his time at Harvard the family was in England. Kennedy graduated *cum laude* from Harvard in 1940.

In the fall of 1940 Kennedy spent several weeks at Stanford University Graduate School. That same year his first book was published. *Why England Slept* told of the years leading up to World War II. The book's main theme was England's unreadiness for the war. It was an expanded version of Kennedy's senior-year thesis at Harvard. Kennedy donated some of the proceeds from the sales to the war-torn city of Plymouth, England.

Such a large family needed a getaway. And Joseph Kennedy found it on Cape Cod. The Kennedy compound is a group of houses in Hyannisport, Massachusetts. There are three family homes facing one of the town's quiet, tree-lined streets. Situated near the ocean, the center house belonged to Jack's father. Behind the houses, the backyards stretch gently down to a private beach on the Atlantic Ocean. The compound has provided the perfect family retreat for many years.

The Kennedy family, always closely knit, has been struck by tragedy on many occasions. Joseph P. Kennedy, Jr., Jack's older brother, was killed during World War II. Sister Kathleen died in a plane crash in 1948. And sister Rosemary, born retarded, has lived in an institution for most of her life. Brother Robert F. Kennedy was assassinated in Los Angeles in 1968.

And Ted Kennedy's political career suffered when he was involved in an accident that proved fatal to a Kennedy staffer, Mary Jo Kopechne. In 1969 his car, in which they were both riding, went off a bridge in Chappaquiddick, not far from the Kennedy compound on Cape Cod. Kennedy disappeared for a few crucial hours after the accident. As a result, many people think he acted irresponsibly. They think he might have been in some way responsible for the young woman's death.

The Kennedy clan at home on their estate in Hyannisport, Massachusetts

JFK in World War II

Jack Kennedy sensed that America's involvement in World War II was inevitable. So he enlisted in the U.S. Navy even before America went to war. In the fall of 1941, he was commissioned as an ensign. But it was not until the following year that Kennedy was called up for active duty. He was assigned to attend PT-boat training school.

In March 1943 Kennedy sailed for the South Pacific. In April, as lieutenant junior grade, he took command of PT 109 in the Solomon Islands.

On August 2, 1943, the Japanese destroyer *Amugiri* rammed PT 109, slicing it in two. Two crew members drowned when they went down with the boat's rear section. Kennedy received a serious back injury when the force of the impact hurled him against the back wall of the cockpit. The blow aggravated an injury Kennedy had received playing football in school. The back injury would plague Kennedy the rest of his life.

Still, Kennedy was able to help the survivors. Of the ten other men, only one was badly injured. They clung to the forward section of the ship while it remained afloat. When this part began to sink, Kennedy led the men in a swim to the nearest island. Kennedy himself towed the injured crewman by grasping his life preserver strap during the four-hour swim to the island.

Two days later Kennedy and his crewmen swam two miles to another, larger island. Kennedy again tended to the injured sailor.

Looking for help, the next day Kennedy and one of his men swam to yet another island. There the famished sailors found the wreck of a Japanese vessel. They saw a case of hard candy and crackers. Returning to the main group with some of the food, Kennedy and his companion met some islanders. Kennedy scratched a brief message on a coconut shell and gave it to the islanders. They carried it to Allied forces in the area and a ship came to rescue the party on August 8. In later years Kennedy kept the coconut with the carved message in his office at the White House.

For his bravery in action, Kennedy was decorated with three medals. He received the Navy and Marine Corps Medal as well as the Purple Heart.

Early in 1944 Kennedy returned to the United States. He was suffering from malaria. He was hospitalized both for that and for his back injury. In June 1944 Boston doctors operated on a ruptured disc in Kennedy's spine.

In March 1945 Kennedy was discharged from the navy. He immediately went to work as a reporter for the International News Service. In April he was in San Francisco covering the first meeting of the United Nations in the city. During this same period he edited a privately printed tribute prepared by members of the Kennedy family in memory of their brother Joe, who had been killed in the war.

The Young Jackie

Jacqueline Lee Bouvier was born to John (Black Jack) and Janet Bouvier on July 28, 1929, in Southampton, New York. Her father, a stockbroker, drank to excess and eventually lost his fortune, and his self-respect. The family was staunchly Republican. Her parents' marriage was not a happy one, and they were divorced. Mrs. Bouvier then married Hugh Auchincloss, who raised Jackie and her younger sister, Lee. The girls grew up mostly at the Auchincloss estates in Rhode Island and Virginia.

Despite her parents' unhappy marriage, Jackie's early years were good ones. She was educated first at Miss Porter's School in Farmington, Connecticut. Then she went to Vassar. She received her degree from George Washington University in 1951. She traveled extensively, which broadened her understanding of the world. Jackie was already fluent in French and also spoke Spanish. Some of her ease with languages had been instilled by her mother. Mrs. Auchincloss frequently spent afternoons with her daughters when the three of them spoke only French.

Jacqueline Bouvier was Debutante of the Year in 1947. She became a journalist and photographer. She was earning $42.50 a week from the *Washington Times-Herald* as an "inquiring photographer." In 1953 she went to Great Britain to cover the coronation of Queen Elizabeth II.

It was on one of her photo assignments in Washington in 1952 that Jacqueline Bouvier met John F. Kennedy. He was beginning his political career and she was a promising

John F. Kennedy met the young Jacqueline Lee Bouvier when she was on assignment as a photographer for the Washington Times-Herald.

young photojournalist. Jackie was 12 years and two months younger than Jack.

Their wedding—on September 12, 1953, in Newport, Rhode Island—was one of the great social events of that or any other year. The entire U.S. Senate was invited to the event. Joseph Kennedy more or less took away control of the wedding arrangements from Jackie's mother and step-father. Some 800 people attended the wedding ceremony, and over 1,200 flocked to the reception. And, or course, because it involved a Kennedy, there was heavy press coverage. It was exactly the kind of wedding Jackie and her mother hadn't wanted. The biggest disappointment of the day for Jackie was that her father didn't turn up.

The Road to the White House

Kennedy had to prove he was not just a rich man playing at politics. He had first been elected to the House of Representatives in 1946. He was reelected to the two-year office twice. During those six years, Kennedy earned a reputation as a liberal. He championed the rights of labor unions. He also supported bills for low-cost housing for the poor.

JFK and Jackie waiting on the platform at Union Station to welcome a visiting dignitary

During this period Kennedy perfected his natural ability as a speaker. Jack's Boston accent was considered an asset. He was easy to understand but had just a touch of the exotic and upper class. He impressed listeners both by his eloquence and his sense of conviction. His style was confident, relaxed and sincere. He made a point of quoting great statesmen and writers of the past. As he gained experience as a politician, he became an even better speaker.

In November 1952 Kennedy faced Henry Cabot Lodge for a Massachusetts senate seat. He defeated the incumbent senator by 70,000 votes. Kennedy was to come up against the New England aristocrat once more in 1960. At that time Lodge shared the Republican ticket as Richard Nixon's vice presidential running mate.

Early on Jack learned the value of the Kennedy name in politics. He also discovered ways to use the family to keep himself in the public eye. When Jack's youngest brother, Ted, was still in law school, he was appointed campaign manager of one Massachusetts election. Special television call-in programs were set up for the state's voters. Jackie and the Kennedy sisters manned the phones.

By 1954 Kennedy was in such pain from his back injuries that he could walk only with the help of crutches. In October of that year, and then again in February 1955, he underwent operations to correct his back problems. During his lengthy convalescence, Kennedy began to write a book. It is a study of eight American senators who risked their political careers to support their convictions. Kennedy called the book *Profiles in Courage*. It was published in January 1956. The book won the Pulitzer Prize for biography in 1957. Kennedy is the only president to have won a Pulitzer Prize. The prize has only a small cash award, but it carries a lot of prestige.

In 1956, at the Democratic National Convention in Chicago, Kennedy sought the vice presidential nomination. But he lost out to Tennessee Senator Estes Kefauver. Although he was bitterly disappointed, Kennedy put the defeat to good use. Kennedy always learned from his political mistakes. After all, he was still in his 30s, too young to be seriously considered for the presidency.

Kennedy had other things against him. As well as being considered too young, he didn't have a lot of experience. And, most important of all, he was a Roman Catholic. No Catholic had ever made it to the White House. Another Catholic, Alfred E. Smith, once the governor of New York, had run for the nation's highest office. But that was in 1928, and he had been badly defeated. Had times changed enough?

Joseph Kennedy had planned that his oldest son, Joseph, would one day be president. But after Joe Junior was killed during World War II, the elder Kennedy turned his attention to Jack. He would be the Kennedy who would one day be president.

An avid sailor, JFK spent many hours sailing at the family home in Hyannisport.

JFK campaigning for the vice presidential nomination during the 1956 Democratic National Convention in Chicago

The 1960 Campaign

When Kennedy ran for president, the family fortune was estimated at close to half a billion dollars. Television had become popular, and most of the campaign events were shown across the nation. All the Kennedys pitched in to help Jack's campaign. Rose Kennedy had been born into a political family, so campaigning was second nature to her. Bobby Kennedy was a totally dedicated campaign manager. Like his older brother, Bobby was shrewd and ambitious. Using the family to the hilt was one of the Kennedy strengths.

A principal challenge Kennedy faced was convincing blue-collar workers—in places like West Virginia—that he was in touch with their problems. After all, he came from a background of wealth and privilege. Critics charged that he had crossed the Atlantic more times than he had crossed the Appalachian Mountains.

Kennedy made winning over the West Virginians one of the priorities of his campaign. He gave speeches, shook hands and attended receptions around the state. He finally won the hearts of the people—and their votes.

Jackie Kennedy was aware of this when she chose West Virginia glassware for the White House. She hoped to promote American industry—particularly in parts of the country that were suffering from prolonged economic slumps.

Television came to the fore that fall. The famous Nixon-Kennedy debates took place, sometimes in front of as many as 70 million people. Kennedy's assurance and appeal paid off. With little trouble, he outshone Richard Nixon both as a personality and as a thinker. People remembered the debates. They were very important when Election Day came around.

The 1960 presidential election was held on Tuesday, November 8. It was one of the closest in American history.

There was a heavy voter turnout, since both candidates were immensely popular. But a very small number of votes—some 100,000 out of 69 million—separated the winner from the loser. A few extra votes could have put Nixon in the White House.

Kennedy's victory made him the youngest elected president in history. He was taking over from Dwight D. Eisenhower, at 70 the oldest. Kennedy was also the first president who had been born in the 20th century as well as the first Roman Catholic to hold the office. Shortly after the election, his son, John, Jr., was born. While Jackie was recovering in the hospital, Jack baby-sat for their three-year-old daughter, Caroline, in their home in Washington's Georgetown.

JFK and three-year old Caroline leave their Georgetown home. While Jackie was recovering from the birth of John Jr., the president looked after their daughter.

The Inauguration

John F. Kennedy's inauguration as the 35th president took place on January 20, 1961. It was a bitterly cold, clear day. Because of heavy snowfall in Washington, the inaugural gala the night before had started hours late. Fewer than half the invited guests had arrived by the time marked on their invitations. At 11:30 in the morning Kennedy and retiring President Eisenhower rode together to the Capitol for the ceremony. Chief Justice Earl Warren administered the oath of office. Everything seemed to indicate a successful start to the presidency.

Kennedy's inaugural speech included the following words near the beginning: "The world is very different now. For man holds in his mortal hands the power to abolish all forms of human poverty and all forms of human life."

Theodore Sorensen was one of Kennedy's speech writers. He was largely responsible for the eloquent inaugural address. Kennedy's charge to the nation, "Ask not what your country can do for you; ask what you can do for your country," was almost surely Sorensen's. The final words of the speech, "God's work must truly be our own," brought thunderous applause. The safety and dullness of the Eisenhower years were now past. A new and exciting era had begun.

Poet Robert Frost was present. He had prepared an ode specially written for the event. But there was so much glare from the sun that he recited one of his earlier poems from memory. At one point something unexpected happened—the rostrum caught fire, temporarily knocking out the public-address system.

The Beautiful Couple

The Kennedys were distinct opposites. Jackie seemed refined and graceful. She was knowledgeable about food, wine, art and antiques. Jack had driving ambition. He never declined the chance to advance his career. He had come from a large, united family who enjoyed noise and rough-and-tumble athletics. Where Jack was outgoing and friendly, Jackie could be aloof and distant. She was a private person, not used to the public eye. He, on the other hand, was always a public person.

From the start their courtship had been short on conventional "romance." In fact, because they were both young and busy, it was often difficult for them to find time to be together. In many ways, the family he built in his marriage with Jackie never took the place of the large family he had grown up in.

They developed a way of life that became known as the Kennedy style. It was a combination of intelligence, good taste and sophistication. It was elegant and relaxed, formal and innovative at the same time.

The Kennedys introduced several things to White House entertainments. At large dinners they seated guests at small tables rather than at one large one. Reception lines were dispensed with whenever possible. Menus were simplified

A young and attractive couple, the Kennedys brought grace and elegance to the White House and were favorites of the American public.

to eliminate too many courses. After-dinner entertainment in the East Room was provided by well-known performers. This brought greater attention to the nation's cultural achievements.

There was a feeling of renewal and of hope for a more active and energetic way of life. The whole atmosphere suggested youth and vigor. Indeed if Kennedy was youthful, Mrs. Kennedy seemed almost a child. She was the third youngest of the 29 wives of presidents who had served as first lady since 1789.

When the Kennedys went to France in 1961, Jackie Kennedy was cheered more strongly than Jack Kennedy. She had beauty and charm, not to mention style. The French knew she spoke their language and understood their culture. On that occasion, Jack Kennedy introduced himself: "I'm the man who accompanied Jacqueline Kennedy to Paris, and I've enjoyed it."

Everyone in America wanted to be part of the Kennedy family. They were young, attractive, athletic, stylish and—yes—rich. They had everything. The Kennedys seized the public imagination like nobody before or since.

There was a tremendous sense of family among all the Kennedys. They always got together for birthdays, weddings and anniversaries. And holidays were a special time for parties and other get-togethers.

The Kennedys were always active and politically aware. They were avid readers, both of books and of an assortment of periodicals. They also enjoyed lively discussions of current events.

Despite his enormous wealth, Jack Kennedy almost never carried money with him, always depending on Jackie and their friends. Jack never had money to pay for a cab ride or to pick up a restaurant tab. Exceedingly vain, Jack Kennedy thought a wallet would create an unsightly bulge in his back pocket.

But maybe there was more to it than vanity. Kennedy was accused of not giving Jackie enough money for necessary entertainment expenses. She complained that sometimes food ran short at White House receptions. It was rumored that ice cubes and even wedges of lemons and limes were recirculated among guests at White House parties.

JFK in the Oval Office

Kennedy's term of office was just two months short of three years. He was personally very wealthy. And he had the whole Kennedy family fortune behind him. As president, he donated the whole of his presidential salary to charity. The only other president who had done this was Herbert Hoover.

The Cold War

Kennedy's years in office were marked by the Cold War. That state of tension between the United States and the Soviet Union—between democracy and communism—affected all aspects of foreign policy.

One of the young president's first challenges came in April 1961. The CIA had trained and equipped 1,400 Cuban exiles to spearhead an invasion against Cuba's dictator, Fidel Castro. The military operation was set for the Bay of Pigs on Cuba's south coast. The invasion ended in disaster. Almost 1,200 of the invaders were captured by Castro's forces. Following the invasion, Kennedy tried to figure out what had gone wrong. He even sat down with former President Dwight D. Eisenhower to get his advice. Kennedy humbly assumed full responsibility for the affair even though it had been in the planning stages before he took office.

In 1961 Kennedy also sent over 2,000 military advisers and technicians to Vietnam in support of the American commitment there to prevent the spread of communism.

In October 1962 Kennedy went on national television to warn of a dangerous buildup of Soviet missiles in Cuba. This situation was particularly dangerous because Cuba, only 90 miles off the coast of Florida, could easily attack the United States. Kennedy proposed a strict quarantine on all ships headed for Cuba. Kennedy was pointing a finger specifically at the Soviet Union. Any ships containing weapons destined for Cuba were to be turned back or risk being fired upon. People around the country awoke the morning after the announcement thinking war was imminent. For a week, the world was on the brink of nuclear war. But then the Soviets backed down, removed the weapons, and the Cuban missile crisis passed.

Kennedy also resisted the Soviet buildup in Berlin. He committed increased forces to maintaining the freedom of West Berlin. Berlin had been a divided city since the end of World War II. But in 1961 the Soviets had constructed a dividing wall to prevent people from going to the West. It virtually imprisoned the people of East Berlin. Kennedy visited the Berlin Wall in the summer of 1963. There he delivered his famous *"Ich bin ein Berliner"* ("I am a Berliner") speech. He was saying that all humans were, in some sense, Berliners and shared the city's struggle for freedom.

With the continuation of Cold War tensions a national fallout shelter program was begun in the United States. Thousands of homes around the country were equipped with emergency shelters. The White House was no exception. These shelters were intended to help citizens survive a nuclear attack. Civil defense preparedness was made a national priority.

At the same time that Kennedy worked for peace and an end to the Cold War, he fought to keep American military power strong with increased defense spending.

One of Kennedy's other priorities was supremacy in space. The Soviets had been first, in April 1961, to launch a man into space. The first manned American spaceflight came in May 1961. That month Kennedy approached Congress to ask for funds for the Apollo space program. The goal: to land a man on the moon before the end of the decade.

JFK and Jackie entertain at the 1962 Nobel Prize dinner.

Civil Rights

During Kennedy's administration the civil rights movement began in earnest. Segregation was still a fact of life in the South. Although blacks were encouraged to register to vote, there were attacks on civil rights workers and demonstrators. And black schools and churches were still being burned by some whites. When a black tried to enroll at the University of Mississippi, a riot broke out. The upset left two people dead and hundreds injured, including several hundred marshals sent to maintain order.

In 1963 a civil rights bill was presented. The bill provided for integration of schools. There were to be no more separate schools for blacks. It also guaranteed equal access for all races to restaurants, hotels and retail establishments.

A Liberal President

As president, Kennedy was true to Democratic party ideals—he believed in liberal causes. He fought for increased social security benefits. He raised the minimum wage for workers. He worked toward disarmament and succeeded in getting the Soviet Union, Great Britain and the United States to sign a treaty. It banned atomic testing in the atmosphere, outer space, and underwater.

In March 1961 he established the Peace Corps. Mostly young, idealistic workers and technicians were to be sent to underdeveloped areas to teach people how to be more self-sufficient. The Peace Corps' first project, a road-building program in Tanganyika, was announced in April. By March

1963, more than 5,000 Peace Corps members had been sent to countries around the world.

Kennedy offered the Alliance for Progress program to assist Latin American countries. The plan would help the countries achieve greater economic, social and political stability. And he committed the United States to assist Southeast Asian countries to achieve democracy.

Kennedy also created a federal aid-to-education program in the United States. The sciences were especially encouraged. The physical skills of American schoolchildren were tested nationally. And the results pointed to the need for greater emphasis on physical fitness.

People were also concerned about doing away with religious intolerance. So, also in 1963, the Supreme Court handed down an important, and controversial, decision. It banned prayer in public schools.

President and Mrs. Kennedy leave church after an Easter service.

The first family relaxes with their dogs at Hyannisport.

The Lively
First Family

The Kennedys were one of the most beloved first families. Their lives were completely public. And most of the public wanted to know, to *be* these people.

When the Kennedys came to the White House they were the youngest presidential couple since Theodore and Edith Roosevelt moved in in 1901.

Mrs. Kennedy's priority was a normal life for her children. She deliberately chose to limit her social engagements and her charitable work to devote herself to her children and her husband.

Jacqueline Kennedy gave birth to four children, two of whom died in infancy. One was Patrick Joseph Kennedy, who died two days after he was born in August 1963. Patrick was the first child to be born to a president in office since the 1890s. (Then, Mrs. Grover Cleveland had given birth to two children.) A previous Kennedy child, their first, a daughter, had been stillborn in 1956.

Their other children, Caroline (born in 1957) and John F. Kennedy, Jr. (born in 1960), have matured and are now grown up. Because they are Kennedys, they are still frequently in the news. Caroline is married to Edwin Schlossberg and is a young mother. She is an attorney and in 1991 co-authored a best-selling book about the Bill of Rights. John F. Kennedy, Jr., has recently passed the New York State bar exam and practices law in New York City.

A grown-up Caroline and John, Jr., with their mother, Jackie, and their uncle, Senator Ted Kennedy

The Kennedy children grew up surrounded by the world of nature, horses, sports, books and travel. They were happy living an active life, on beaches or in the open air.

Kennedy was the first president who awakened Americans to the need for physical fitness. Family games of touch football caught the American fancy. And Jack Kennedy was also an avid golfer and sailor. Fifty-mile hikes were popular.

Before the Kennedy children were allowed to sail, family members took them out to sea. The children were then thrown overboard wearing their life preservers. In this way it was hoped they would learn not to panic if they later had to abandon ship.

Because the Kennedy children were so young when they lived at the White House, their parents trimmed their tree on Christmas Eve. And they set up figures of Santa Claus outdoors. One year Jackie Kennedy visited the 200 patients at the District of Columbia children's hospital, distributing gifts.

Pablo Casals was a noted guest at the Kennedy White House. The famous cellist had appeared at the White House when Theodore Roosevelt was president 50 years earlier. This was his second visit.

Kennedy surrounded himself with the best and brightest at all levels of his administration. Pierre Salinger was his press secretary. He was a capable journalist who helped keep the Kennedys in the public eye while at the same time protecting their privacy. And Mrs. Kennedy's social secretary was Letitia Baldrige.

The public couldn't get enough of the Kennedys and

A Kennedy family Christmas

The Kennedys at Camp David, the presidential retreat. Caroline is riding Macaroni.

never tired of reading about the smallest details in their lives. Stories of Jackie's clothing, hairstyles and beauty secrets found their way into magazines, books and on to television and radio programs. Americans followed the antics of Caroline's pony, Macaroni, and her dog, Pushinka, a gift from Soviet Premier Nikita Khrushchev. Even the most mundane happenings sold newspapers and kept the family on page one.

In the family's private quarters Mrs. Kennedy had a special nursery and schoolroom fitted up for Caroline and John-John. Some of Caroline's young playmates joined her for nursery activities. John wasn't even two months old when the Kennedys moved in. But already Caroline was acting out her role as big sister. She would hold him, play with him or push him around in a stroller.

The children grew rapidly in their few short years at the White House, and the whole nation eagerly followed details of Caroline's birthday parties and her Halloween costumes. They also waited for news of John's first tooth, first word and first step. John called his father Foo-Foo Head, and the president's name for him was Bunny Rabbit.

The children delighted the nation and visitors to the White House as well. They were always welcome to play in the president's office, often interrupting important meetings.

The White House Restoration

In February 1962 Mrs. Kennedy gave a television tour of the White House to 60 million viewers. Television cameras showed firsthand where the nation's president and his family lived. A whole nation sat transfixed when Mrs. Kennedy opened the White House to the public. Never before had the executive mansion been seen by so many people at one time.

The cameras also showed the transformation that Jacqueline Kennedy had made in the decoration of the White House. She restored it once more to dignity and historical authenticity. Jacqueline knew her furniture and historical periods. Most of all, she had style.

Mrs. Kennedy had begun by scouring White House records and the contents of storage rooms. She was looking for information about authentic pieces for furnishing the White House. Jackie formed the Fine Arts Committee for the White House to help locate the best examples of art and furniture. She believed that "everything in the White House must have a reason for being there."

President Kennedy's desk was rescued from the White House basement. The beautifully carved piece had been put together nearly a hundred years earlier from the oak timbers of the British frigate *Resolute*. It had been a gift to President Rutherford Hayes from Queen Victoria.

A Typical Day

At 7:30 each morning, the Kennedys were awakened by a servant. He brought them a breakfast tray and several morning papers. He also brought any messages that might have arrived during the night.

While Jackie and Jack had breakfast, Caroline and young John rushed in, turned on the television and watched cartoons. With the sound near full blast, this went on for nearly an hour. The president read and chatted or played around with the children as he dressed.

A little after 9, Kennedy would walk over to his office in the West Wing of the White House. Often he was accompanied by at least one of the children. He worked all morning and then generally took a brief swim just before lunchtime. Usually he ate alone or with Jackie. Only rarely were there lunch guests.

JFK listens to the young Caroline.

After lunch, Kennedy put on pajamas and took a 45-minute nap. Both the swim and nap—on a heating pad—were to help relieve Kennedy's back pain. While he was getting dressed after his nap, Kennedy would talk with Jackie. In the afternoon, he generally had appointments, either in the West Wing or in the White House family quarters.

Kennedy worked until 7:30 or 8 at night. Then came dinner with Jackie and relaxation. Often, however, there were social engagements on the agenda. Unless there were formal arrangements, the Kennedys seldom went out. Small dinners of less than ten were frequent, and there were, of course, occasional state dinners with much larger numbers. Jackie liked to keep evenings as free as possible. And she always tried to make everything lighthearted and enjoyable, no matter where they were.

Kennedy's Oval Office rocking chair became a major symbol of his presidency. But it was more a necessity—to relieve his almost constant back pain—than anything else. The rocking chair helped somewhat, as did a cloth back brace Kennedy wore under his suit. According to his sister Eunice, Kennedy was never good at relaxing, "but Jackie has gone a long way to change that."

The Funeral

It was partly the horror of the assassination. It was partly the fact that it all appeared on national television. And it was mostly because the country cared deeply for the Kennedys that the weekend in November 1963 was such a moving time for most Americans.

The Monday after the assassination was a day of national mourning. People sat glued to their television sets. They watched the sad, slow procession from the Capitol to the funeral at Washington's St. Matthew's Cathedral. That was followed by the military parade to the grave site at Arlington National Cemetery.

Mrs. Kennedy requested that her husband's funeral arrangements duplicate many of the features of Abraham Lincoln's funeral in 1865. After being flown back to Washington from Texas, the president's casket rested on a black-draped platform. Patterned after Lincoln's, the coffin was placed in the candlelit East Room of the White House. An honor guard kept vigil. Doorways, windows, mirrors, chandeliers and even fireplaces were draped in black.

The Kennedy family at the funeral of JFK

In a moving gesture, young John, Jr., salutes his father during the funeral ceremony.

Later the president's body was carried on a black caisson drawn by six gray horses. Taken to the Capitol rotunda on Sunday, November 24, the body lay in state there until the actual funeral procession.

Heads of state and high-ranking representatives from more than 100 countries came to Washington for Kennedy's funeral. People the world over mourned his passing.

But the image many people have taken with them from that awful day is one of Kennedy's son, John F. Kennedy, Jr. Watching his father's coffin pass by, he gave a military salute. Too young to comprehend the dreadfulness of the event, he is stoically present, a vital image of young America. It was his third birthday.

The Legacy of JFK

In the aftermath of the assassination, a stunned nation sought to honor the leader it had lost. People all over the country named roads, highways, schools and other public buildings after him. For several years, the NASA space center in Florida was called Cape Kennedy. But the original name—Cape Canaveral—has been restored.

Washington, D.C., has been enriched through the John F. Kennedy Center for the Performing Arts. There the finest performers from around the world present theater, dance and opera. The center draws visitors not only from Washington but from all parts of the country and world.

And, near Boston, on the banks of the Charles River, the JFK Library has been built. An archive and research center, it is dedicated primarily to students interested in Kennedy and the Kennedy years. At nearby Harvard University there is also the John F. Kennedy School of Government. It is set in the midst of Harvard buildings Kennedy knew as a student.

Jackie After JFK

Five years after Kennedy's assassination, Jackie married the wealthy Greek tycoon Aristotle Onassis, whose name she still bears. Mrs. Kennedy was only the second first lady to remarry. (Frances Cleveland had been the first.) Partly because of the Kennedy aura, her act drew much criticism. Onassis died in 1975, leaving Jackie a widow once more. Mrs. Onassis lives in New York City. Since the early 1970s, she has pursued a successful publishing career. Jackie is often seen at artistic and theatrical events. She also lends support to her favorite cause—architectural preservation. Although almost 30 years have passed since her time at the White House, Mrs. Onassis is still very much a trendsetter.

Jackie at her wedding to Aristotle Onassis

The King and Queen of Camelot

Camelot

During the Kennedy administration, the popular musical *Camelot* was playing in New York. It was Jack Kennedy's favorite musical. He used to play the record over and over. He especially liked the words that ended the title song. Because of this the administration came to be known as Camelot. This was a reference to King Arthur's shining city. King Arthur was the legendary wise and virtuous leader of the ancient Britons. At Camelot he lived in splendor surrounded by his noble knights.

Kennedy liked to think he was a leader like King Arthur. He had a lovely and elegant wife. He had two delightful children. He surrounded himself with a staff of the best and ablest advisers. It was a time of relative peace and stability, with respect for human dignity and artistic achievement. Many people thought it was a time similar to King Arthur's day.

Some critics say that Kennedy failed to accomplish anything of importance during his short term as president. But anyone who lived through the Kennedy years remembers that it was a wonderful time to be an American. Both Jackie and Jack had a vigor and verve that the whole nation felt. The word "charisma" was often used to describe Kennedy's charm and popularity. Kennedy was a leader who had a personal magic that aroused great loyalty and enthusiasm.

There was a belief that the United States could accomplish anything, reach any goal, solve any problem. Kennedy's policies helped to foster this belief. But more than that, the nation felt that it had a true leader, someone the people could trust and be proud of—a president who would help them reach the stars.

For Further Reading

Anthony, Carl Sferrazza. *First Ladies: The Saga of the Presidents' Wives and Their Power, 1789–1961*. New York: William Morrow & Company, 1990.

Fisher, Leonard Everett. *The White House*. New York: Holiday House, 1989.

Friedel, Frank. *The Presidents of the United States of America*. Revised edition. Washington, D.C.: The White House Historical Association, 1989.

Klapthor, Margaret Brown. *The First Ladies*. Revised edition. Washington, D.C.: The White House Historical Association, 1989.

Lindsay, Rae. *The Presidents' First Ladies*. New York: Franklin Watts, 1989.

The Living White House. Revised edition. Washington, D.C.: The White House Historical Association, 1987.

Lowe, Jacques, and Wilfrid Sheed. *The Kennedy Legacy: A Generation Later*. New York: Viking Studio Books, 1988.

Manchester, William. *One Brief Shining Moment: Remembering Kennedy*. Boston: Little, Brown and Company, 1983.

Mills, Judie. *John F. Kennedy*. New York: Franklin Watts, 1988.

St. George, Judith. *The White House: Cornerstone of a Nation*. New York: G. P. Putnam's Sons, 1990.

Shaw, Mark. *The John F. Kennedys: A Family Album*. New York: Greenwich House (a division of Crown Publishers), 1983.

Taylor, Tim. *The Book of Presidents*. New York: Arno Press (a *New York Times* company), 1972.

United Press International and American Heritage. *Four Days: The Historical Record of the Death of President Kennedy.* American Heritage Publishing Company, 1964.

The White House. Washington, D.C.: The White House Historical Association, 1987.

Wolff, Perry. *A Tour of the White House with Mrs. John F. Kennedy.* Garden City, NY: Doubleday & Company, 1962.

Index

Alliance for Progress 29
Apollo space program 27
Arlington National Cemetary 38
Auchincloss, Hugh 12

Baldrige, Leticia 32
Bay of Pigs 25
Berlin 26
Berlin Wall 26
Boston 6
Bouvier, (Black Jack) John 12
Bouvier, Janet 12
Bouvier, Lee 12
Brookline, Massachusetts 6, 7

Camelot 43
Cape Canaveral 41
Cape Cod 8
Cape Kennedy 41
Capitol, the 21, 38, 40
Casals, Pablo 32
Castro, Fidel 25
Chappaquiddick 8
Chicago 6
Choate 7
CIA 25
civil rights 28
Cleveland, Mrs. Grover (Frances) 31, 41
Cold War 25, 26, 27
Congress 27
Cuba 25, 26

Dallas 5

East Berlin 26
East Room 23, 38
Eisenhower, Dwight D. 20, 21, 25

Fine Arts Committee for the White
    House 36
Fitzgerald, John F. (Honey Fitz) 6
France 23

Frost, Robert 21
George Washington University 12
Georgetown 20
Great Britain 28

Harvard University 7, 41
Hayes, Rutherford 36
House of Representatives 14
Hoover, Herbert 25
Hyannisport 8

International News Service 11

JFK Library 41
John F. Kennedy Center for the
    Performing Arts 41
John F. Kennedy School of
    Government 41

Kefauver, Estes 16
Kennedy, Caroline 20, 31, 34, 35
Kennedy, Edward (Ted) 6, 8, 15
Kennedy, Eunice 6, 38
Kennedy, Jacqueline Lee (Bouvier) 5,
    12, 13, 15, 19, 20, 22, 23, 24, 30, 31,
    32, 34, 35, 36, 37, 38, 41, 42, 44
Kennedy, Jean 6
Kennedy, John Fitzgerald 5, 6, 7, 8, 10,
    11, 12, 14, 15, 16, 18, 19, 20, 21, 22,
    23, 24, 25, 26, 27, 28, 29, 30, 32, 36,
    37, 38, 40, 41, 43, 44
Kennedy, John Fitzgerald, Jr. 20, 31,
    34, 35, 40
Kennedy, Joseph Patrick 6, 8, 13, 16
Kennedy, Joseph, Jr. 6, 8, 11, 16
Kennedy, Kathleen 6, 8
Kennedy, Patricia 6
Kennedy, Patrick 6
Kennedy, Patrick Joseph 31
Kennedy, Robert F. 6, 8, 19
Kennedy, Rose Fitzgerald 6, 7, 18
Kennedy, Rosemary 6, 8

Khrushchev, Nikita 34
Kopechne, Mary Jo 8

Lincoln, Abraham 38
Lodge, Henry Cabot 15
London 6

Newport, Rhode Island 13
Nixon-Kennedy debates 19
Nixon, Richard M. 15, 19, 20

Onassis, Aristotle 41
Oval Office 38

Peace Corps 28, 29
Princeton 7
Profiles in Courage 15
PT 109 10
Pulitzer Prize 16

Riverdale 7
Roosevelt, Edith 30
Roosevelt, Theodore 30, 32

Salinger, Pierre 32
San Francisco 11
Schlossberg, Edwin 31
Smith, Alfred E. 16
Sorensen, Theodore 21
Southeast Asia 29
Soviet Union 26, 28
Stanford University 7
Supreme Court 29

Tanganyika 28

United Nations 11

Vassar 12
Victoria, Queen of England 36
Vietnam 25

Warren, Earl 21
Washington, D.C. 40
West Berlin 26
West Wing 36, 37
While England Slept 7
White House 7, 20, 22, 24, 26, 30, 35, 36,
    37, 38, 42